WOOSAH
WORKPLACE PEACE

A WORKBOOK & JOURNAL FOR WOMEN OF COLOR

7 KEYS TO OBTAINING A MORE FULFILLING WORK EXPERIENCE

RAHKAL C. D. SHELTON

Copyright © 2022 by Be The Inspired You

All rights reserved. This book or any portion thereof may not be reproduced or used in any manner whatsoever without the express written permission of the publisher.

Printed in the United States of America

ISBN: 978-1-7376892-3-2

Rahkal C. D. Shelton
Be The Inspired You

Woosah
www.rahkalshelton.com

Instagram: @woosahthebook @betheinspiredyou @rcarladanille

Cover Illustration: Nancy Devard

CONTENTS

ABOUT THE AUTHOR

INTRODUCTION

IDENTIFYING & OWNING PURPOSE — 11
DISCOVERING WHAT YOU'RE HERE FOR AND WHAT YOU REALLY WANT

UNDERSTANDING THE PLAYING FIELD — 22
TYPES OF ADVERSITIES WOC FACE IN THE WORKPLACE

YOU ARE ON THE MENU — 33
STOP FIGHTING FOR A SEAT AT THE TABLE AND START SERVING YOU

NAVIGATING WITH GRACE — 46
TOXIC ENVIRONMENTS, STRESS MANAGEMENT, AND BOUNDARY SETTING

COMMUNITIES, TRIBES & NETWORKING — 76
JOIN THEM, SEEK THEM, BUILD THEM

GOALDIGGER — 87
GOAL SETTING AND TOOLS TO THRIVE

THE MOVE (GETTING TO WERK) — 110
WRITING YOUR CAREER PLAN AND VISION

ENDNOTE — 130

ABOUT THE AUTHOR

Featured in Forbes, HuffPost Rahkal Shelton Roberson is a multi-talented author, dynamic speaker, certified professional coach, skilled educator, and CEO of Be The Inspired You, LLC, a personal and professional development lifestyle brand.

With over 15 years of combined experience in broadcast, project management, and education, Rahkal leverages her professional problem-solving, critical thinking, and strategic planning skills with her knack for creativity, solutions, and passion for serving women.

@rcarladanielle
@woosahthebook
@betheinspiredyou

Her uncanny ability to connect and encourage is the foundation of her mission: serving, inspiring, and helping individuals confidently identify, own, and live out their God-given purpose. Rahkal works with organizations and individuals to develop talent and break free of self-imposed restrictions while cultivating harmony and strategy to live more significantly.

She is the author of Woosah: A Survival Guide for Women of Color Working In Corporate, Dreams Bigger Than Texas: A Story of Faith, Purpose, Perseverance, and Growth Into Womanhood, and Blackbird: The Story of a SistaMom.

She and her incredible husband live in Atlanta and are the founders of Our Fatherless Foundation, a 501(c)(3) created to help end fatherlessness one family at a time.

—Coach Rahk Roberson

INTRODUCTION

WHAT IS WOOSAH IS ALL ABOUT

/wōo/sah :
deep breath, or sigh. Speaks to gathering yourself and resetting (verb).

Sis, every job you've had, considered, or will take reflects who you are, where you're going, and what you're becoming. Think about it, our careers, college studies, professions, and vocations helps to define us in some way or another. We choose jobs and schools based on our talents or desires.

Whether it's the prestige associated with an Ivy League, the grit earned from an HBCU, taking orders, sweeping floors, cozy cubicles, or a golden ticket corner office with breathtaking views in an executive suite, we all end up somewhere.

The gigs, workplaces we frequent, and hours spent creating, negotiating, and even applying for jobs take us away from what matters most — our loved ones.

However, work is essential; for some, it's defining, and for most, it pays the bills. It's our livelihoods, the means to an end, and the resource that funds travel, our children's education, shopping, and life's pleasantries.

At the same, our jobs and workplaces often enslave us into trading in our valuable time for money, benefits, status, titles, and the comfort of a steady paycheck. Therefore, keeping a foothold on our necks and creating more room for idolizing the all-mighty dollar.

That's enough to make us all Woosah!

INTRODUCTION

Welp, we do have to work for a living, and since we do, why not make it enjoyable? Why not intentionally use our jobs and education as resources to fund or help discover what we really want?
After graduating college, I wish I had had a guide or manual before or shortly after I started my career, specifically in the broadcast industry. But, no...I had nothing to warn me about what I was really entering into. I had no clue what to expect or what working in that environment—as a black woman—would genuinely entail. I thought my internships, experience, and possession of a graduate degree meant something and that it would ultimately help me advance up the corporate ladder. Sadly, I was wrong—so wrong.

As a first-generation college grad and the first in my family to work for large companies and in corporate, male-white-dominated settings, there was so much that I wasn't aware of. For example, I learned that there was an expectation for me to be docile while simultaneously appearing open and inviting in many of my workplaces.

I needed to keep a smile plastered on my face and speak in pleasant, non-confrontational tones. I was expected to passively share my feedback—after others had already spoken, of course, to avoid being labeled "aggressive" or an "angry black woman." Every cell in my body needed to scream, "I'm safe!" to make my employers and colleagues feel more comfortable around me.

I had to be mindful of the optics of my hair and attire, learn to play the game, and filter through passive condescending jabs while being gaslighted and underpaid. I didn't know the importance of boundaries. The answer was always "yes" to my team, bosses, and coworkers. It was exhausting and often left me burned out and questioning my skills and intelligence. Many times, I thought it was me and that I was tripping.

INTRODUCTION

What am I talking about? I'm talking about the painful experiences of discrimination, unconscious and implicit biases, and systematic issues rooted in hate. I'm talking about our country's bitter battle with racism and how it hovers in most workplaces.

Racism is one of those things that we just can't stay silent about, pretend it never happens or that it's over. Hate is the root of racism, and racism infiltrates our workplaces, classrooms, courtrooms, and boardrooms. It's a sickening disease that only causes pain, division, and missed opportunities to see each other's humanity. However, I am hopeful that racism can be cured with love, healthy conversations, kindness, open hearts, and empathetic gestures over time. Addressing racism doesn't have to be divisive. And just because something isn't your experience doesn't mean it isn't someone else's experience. Talking about it with positive intent and solution-based approaches helps to eradicate complicities.

I wrote this companion book to accompany Woosah: A Survival Guide for Women of Color Working In Corporate with the hopes of encouraging healthy dialogue to educate, inspire, provide a voice, and validate an underserved group of women. I also wanted Woosah to serve as a primer for younger women of color, specifically first-gen college-educated black women entering the workforce.

Garnered features in Forbes, HuffPost, and on WGNtv, Woosah continues to inspire women to be more confident in their diverse authenticity while speaking up and protecting their peace. This workbook is designed to do something similar but focuses more on strategies and is tailored to help with brainstorming, planning, and executing clear strategies to obtain workplace fulfillment.

INTRODUCTION

After over 12 years with multiple companies, personally, I had enough of the burnout, microaggression, and being overlooked for opportunities (I was most qualified for). So I made my grand exit from corporate, firing my employer.

As I left, I vowed to educate and empower other women with similar experiences and those preparing to begin their professional journey. Hey, work environments can be stressful all by themselves, so the added pressures that women of color face only worsen matters.

Sis, I want you well, thriving, and confidently identifying and owning your God-given purpose in and out of the workplace. I pray this book helps you get organized, be more intentional, and prepared to thrive professionally. If you commit to doing the work, you'll see transformational results.

Lastly, to accompany this workbook, remember to grab your copy of Woosah: A Survival Guide for Women of Color Working In Corporate.

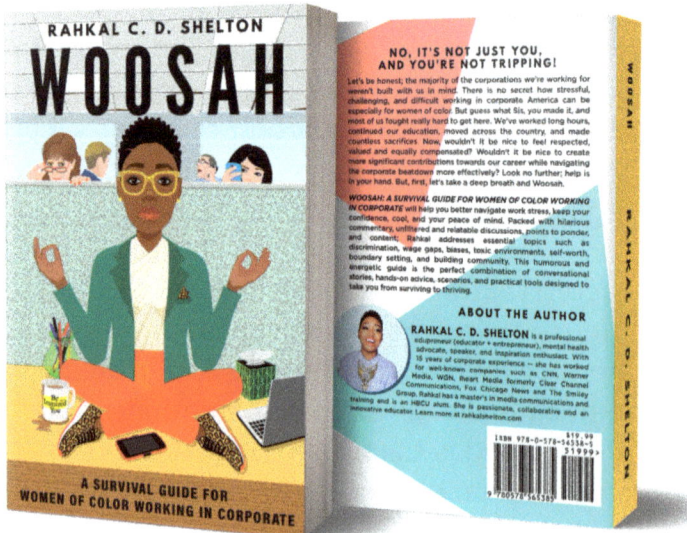

SIS, YOU READY? LET'S GET INTO IT...

7 KEYS TO OBTAINING A MORE FULFILLING WORK EXPERIENCE

- **KNOW YOUR PURPOSE**

- **KNOW WHAT YOU WANT**

- **KNOW WHERE YOU WANNA BE**

KEY #1

SELF-AWARENESS PROVIDE CLARITY AND INTENTIONAL FOCUS.

WHAT DO YOU REALLY WANT?

IDENTIFYING & OWNING PURPOSE

Hey sis! If you haven't heard this lately, or at all, you were made for something great! You are a unique solution to a problem, and the diversity that you bring to your workplace is magical!

Your authenticity, quirks, humor, background, perspective, and talents were given to you on purpose, and they are valuable!

When you aren't your authentic self, your workplace loses an opportunity to learn from you—i.e., your perspective and ideas.

Your background has led you to this point, and because of it, you have profound knowledge, a new approach, and fresh strategies.

Girl, why suppress this?

Furthermore, you were created on purpose and with purpose. And a part of my purpose is to support you with identifying and owning yours. My goal is to help you obtain a more rewarding work experience.

Knowing your purpose can certainly help you. Purpose is the reason for which something is done or created or for which something exists. And what I know about purpose is that living on purpose and with purpose helps reduce anxiety, hopelessness, fear, unfulfillment, and depression.

Think about it; you weren't created to shrink back, play small, burn out, work every day, pay bills and then die. You were created to do good work.

So, give yourself permission to dream, explore, and think about what you really want.

PURPOSE DISCOVERY ACTIVITY

Below are some 'pondering' questions to stimulate your thinking and help you discover your purpose and desires. These questions will not instantaneously reveal your purpose, but they'll help get you thinking and motivated to find it.

Sometimes just writing it out helps to see better.

WHAT ARE YOU PASSIONATE / CARE ABOUT?

- [ ] _____
- [ ] _____
- [ ] _____

WHAT INTEREST & MOTIVATES YOU?

- [ ] _____
- [ ] _____
- [ ] _____

WHAT ARE SOME OF YOUR GIFTS, TALENTS & SKILLS?
(what would your friends and family say these are?)

- [ ] _____
- [ ] _____
- [ ] _____

WHAT WOULD YOU DO FOR FREE?

- [ ] _____
- [ ] _____
- [ ] _____

WHAT DO YOU REALLY WANT?

He who began a good work in you will carry it on to completion
-Philippians 1:6

WHAT DO YOU BELIEVE YOUR PURPOSE IS?

_____
_____
_____
_____
_____
_____
_____
_____
_____
_____
_____
_____
_____
_____
_____
_____
_____
_____

WHAT DO YOU REALLY WANT?

WHAT IS YOUR DREAM JOB/CAREER/OPPORTUNITY?

(Give yourself permission to speak it, write it and to dream big.)

_____
_____
_____
_____
_____
_____
_____
_____
_____
_____
_____
_____
_____
_____
_____

WHAT DO YOU REALLY WANT?

WHAT IS THAT THING YOU'RE INTERESTED IN EXPLORING OR DOING THAT YOU'RE AFRAID OF (AND IT KEEPS COMING BACK UP)?

_____
_____
_____
_____
_____
_____
_____
_____
_____
_____
_____
_____
_____
_____
_____
_____

WHAT DO YOU REALLY WANT?

IS WHAT YOU'RE DOING (PROFESSIONALLY) GETTING YOU CLOSER TO OR FURTHER AWAY FROM YOUR DREAM? HOW?

(If further away, what are you going to do about it?)

_____
_____
_____
_____
_____
_____
_____
_____
_____
_____
_____
_____
_____
_____
_____
_____
_____

WHAT DO YOU REALLY WANT?

ARE YOU SATISFIED WITH YOUR JOB? IF NOT, WHAT CAN YOU LEARN (IN THE MEANTIME) TO SERVE AS A STEPPING STONE FOR YOUR NEXT JOB?

(If not satisfied, what are you going to do about it?)

SPEAK, SIS. SPEAK!
notes

SPEAK, SIS. SPEAK!

notes

SPEAK, SIS. SPEAK!

notes

7 KEYS TO OBTAINING A MORE FULFILLING WORK EXPERIENCE

KNOW WHAT YOU'RE UP AGAINST

KEY #2

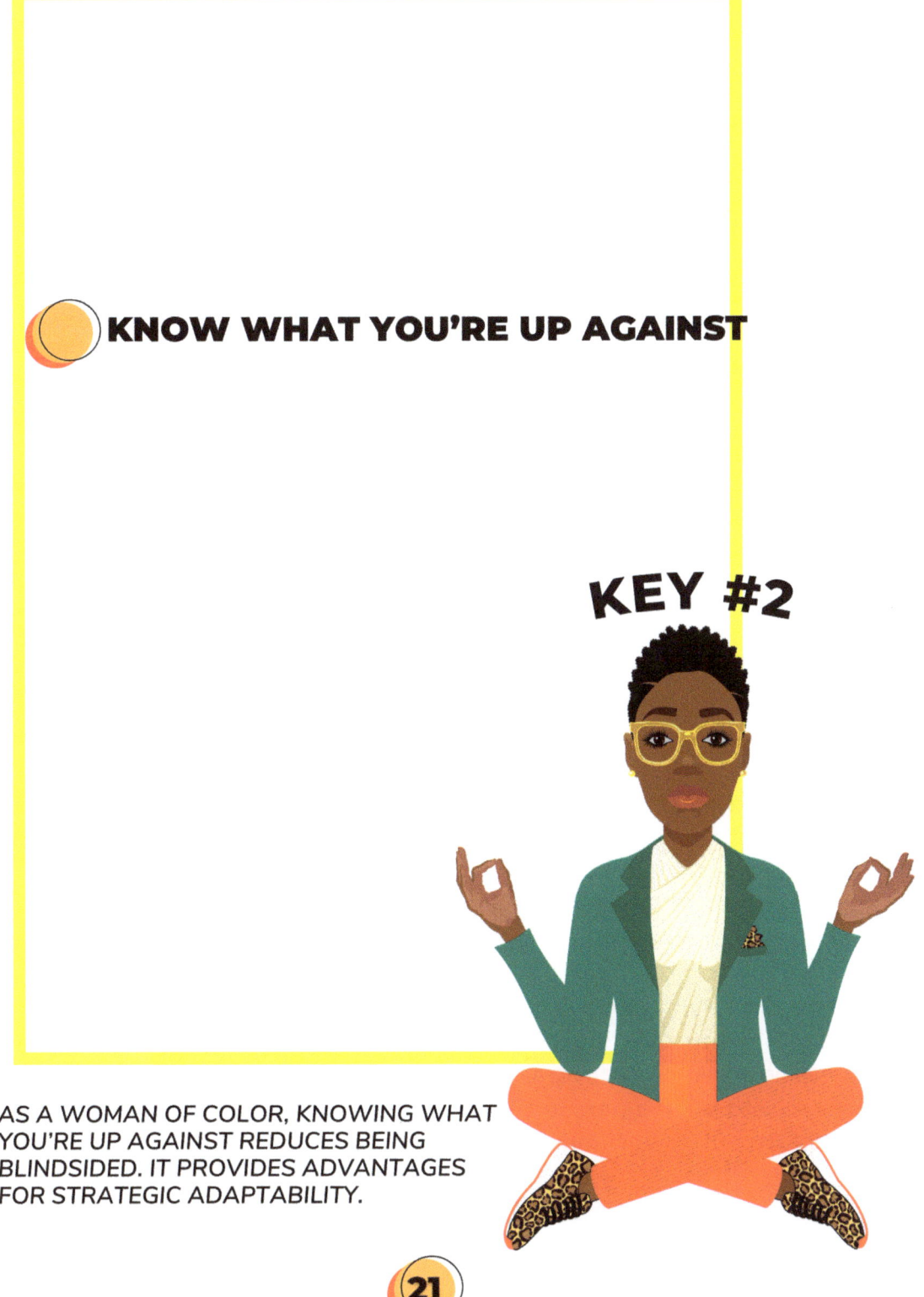

AS A WOMAN OF COLOR, KNOWING WHAT YOU'RE UP AGAINST REDUCES BEING BLINDSIDED. IT PROVIDES ADVANTAGES FOR STRATEGIC ADAPTABILITY.

Derived from Chapter 2 in Woosah

WHAT WE'RE UP AGAINST

THE PLAYING FIELD

The playing field speaks to identifying the landscape and culture of where you're working.

Speaking of landscapes, a couple of inherited constants make the playing field for black and brown women more challenging to navigate than for others. These constants include discrimination, unconscious bias, gender gaps, systematic racism, educational inadequacies, and income/wealth gaps. Let's explore what they mean.

RACIAL & COLOR DISCRIMINATION

The US Equal Employment Opportunity Commission defines racial and color discrimination as treating people such as applicants or employees unfavorably because he or she is of a certain race or because of personal characteristics associated with a specific race—i.e., hair texture, skin color, and/or certain facial features.

Color discrimination involves treating a person unfavorably because of his or her skin color. Race and color discrimination also involves treating a person unfavorably because he or she is married to (or associated with) a person of a particular race or color (US Equal Employment Opportunity Commission, 2019).

WHAT WE'RE UP AGAINST

UNCONSCIOUS/IMPLICIT BIASES

The difference between racial discrimination and unconscious bias is the subtlety and the fact that these biases are unintentional.

Unconscious bias is automatic. They are subconscious prejudices that have been learned, stereotypes, and invalid judgments against a person or group. Unintentional biases are also deeply rooted and influential toward behaviors.

THE GENDER GAP & SYSTEMATIC RACISM

The gender pay gap is the difference between men's and women's salaries. Now, think about how this gap may impact brown and black women. Many, if not most, women of color experience racism and sexism simultaneously. As a result, we are often forced to attain advanced degrees and more extensive experience to boost our chances of snagging higher-paying jobs or advancing in our current positions.

Why? Well, first, it is important to examine and discuss the definition of systematic racism. Systematic racism, in the simplest form, is the impact of all the racist ideas, policies, laws, practices, and rules that our country was founded on now trickled down into present-day standards within society, organizations, and institutions.

> See page 33 in Woosah for detailed examples

WHAT WE'RE UP AGAINST

THE INCOME GAP

The income gap refers to the "gap" in earnings between two groups, such as working whites and blacks. There is also the "wealth gap." However, this gap differs from the income gap because the wealth gap refers to assets minus debts instead of just income alone. These gaps have larger ramifications which, over time, add up to millions of dollars lost in Black and Brown communities.

Be sure to read chapter two of Woosah: A Survival Guide for Women of Color Working In Corporate as it gives a more detailed breakdown with examples of the playing field.

According to LeanIn.org, on average Black women in the United States are paid 36% less than white men and 12% less than white women.

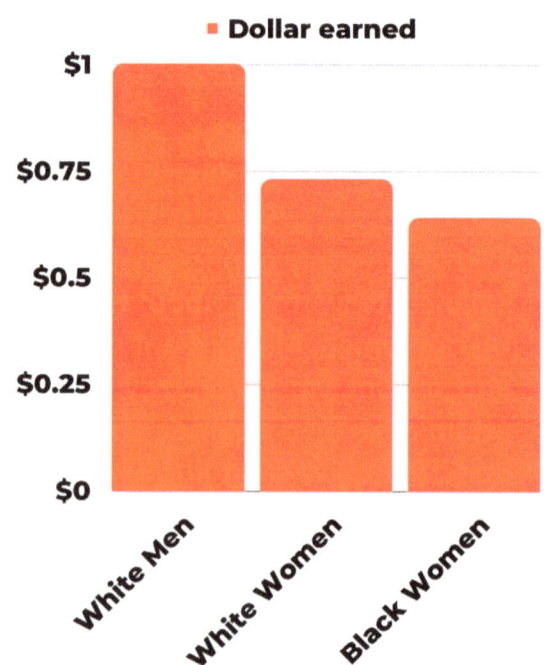

CITATION:
LeanIn.org. (2022). Black women aren't paid fairly. Retrieved from https://leanin.org/data-about-the-gender-pay-gap-for-black-women#!

PLAYING FIELD
ASSESSMENT

		YES	NO
1	Are there black and brown people in leadership positions in your place of employment?	☐	☐

How many? _____

2	Do you feel advocated for by your supervisors?	☐	☐
3	Do you feel you're fairly compensated?	☐	☐

What is the average pay range for your title? _____

4	Have you witnessed or experienced any discrimination throughout your career?	☐	☐
5	Do you feel that your work environment celebrates and supports black and brown women?	☐	☐
6	Have you witnessed others less qualified than you receive promotions or additional work perks / assignments / opportunities?	☐	☐
7	Are you satisfied with your work's culture?	☐	☐
8	Do you feel the need to be extra engaging and really upbeat around your team to avoid feeling misunderstood?	☐	☐
9	Do you feel that leadership cares about you as a person and your professional development?	☐	☐

PLAYING FIELD
ACTION PLAN

STEP ONE

BE AND BRING YOUR AUTHENTIC SELF TO WORK DAILY, WHETHER YOU FEEL YOU'LL BE MISUNDERSTOOD OR NOT. LOOK FOR WAYS TO CONNECT WITH OTHERS AND OWN THE DIVERSITY THAT YOU BRING!

STEP TWO

LOOK FOR OPPORTUNITIES TO SPOTLIGHT AND SHOWCASE YOUR WORK. INTENTIONALLY SHARE WHAT YOU'RE UP TO AND YOUR ACCOMPLISHMENTS WITH THE TEAM AND LEADERSHIP.

STEP THREE

EVALUATE YOUR ROLES AND RESPONSIBILITIES YEARLY TO ENSURE YOUR COMPENSATION REFLECTS YOUR DUTIES.

STEP FOUR

JOT DOWN ALL OBSERVATIONS OF DISCRIMINATION, POWER ABUSE, MICROAGGRESSION, OR UNFAIR TREATMENT. KEEP A RECORD AND EMAIL INSTANCES TO YOURSELF TO KEEP A TIMESTAMP. INCLUDE NAMES, DATES, WITNESSES, ETC., IF YOU NEED TO USE THIS.

PLAYING FIELD
ACTION PLAN

STEP FIVE

DON'T BE AFRAID TO SPEAK UP AND DISRUPT BEHAVIORS THAT ARE IMPEDING ON YOUR PROFESSIONAL DEVELOPMENT. ALSO, DON'T BE AFRAID TO ENGAGE LEADERSHIP IN CONVERSATION, BRINGING YOUR OBSERVATIONS TO THEIR ATTENTION.

STEP SIX

VERIFY WITH HR WHETHER YOU ARE ON THE HIGHER OR LOWER-PAID END OF YOUR PAY RANGE. LINKEDIN, PAYSCALE, INDEED, AND SALARY.COM ARE EXCELLENT REFERENCES.

STEP SEVEN

RESEARCH CERTIFICATIONS, COURSES, AND WAYS TO INCREASE YOUR WORTH.

STEP EIGHT

THINK OF THREE ACCOMPLISHMENTS, SKILLS, OR SUPPORTING POINTS TO SHARE WHEN ASKING FOR A RAISE.

ASK FOR MORE MONEY!

CREATING WEALTH STRATEGIES

We were all created with unique giftings and talents. These gifts and talents are innate; we were born with them and shine in these areas naturally. Because we all have gifts, this proves we're all good at something!

We will dive deeper into this later. For now, I want you to get creative.

Sidebar, many women of color are disenfranchised regarding fair compensation. Therefore not only is negotiating a higher salary essential, but so is having side hustles and the ability to monetize your gifts and talents.

Creating multiple income streams is necessary to help close some of the existing wealth gaps and for your overall well-being.

Let's take an inventory of what you can do to bring in more income. Use the next page for additional space.

THINGS I'M GOOD AT:

_____

_____

_____

POTENTIAL SIDE HUSTLES:

_____

_____

_____

WHO I CAN PARTNER WITH?

_____

_____

_____

WAYS I CAN LEVERAGE THESE TO BUILD WEALTH

_____

_____

_____

SPEAK, SIS. SPEAK!

notes

SPEAK, SIS. SPEAK!
notes

SPEAK, SIS. SPEAK!

notes

7 KEYS TO OBTAINING A MORE FULFILLING WORK EXPERIENCE

KNOW THAT YOU ARE ON THE MENU AND THE PRIZE!

KEY #3

KNOWING WHAT YOU OFFER AND THAT YOU ARE ON THE MENU REDUCES SETTLING AND SHORT-CHANGING YOURSELF. THERE IS FREEDOM IN BEING AUTHENTICALLY YOU IN THE WORKPLACE.

Read along Chapter 3 in Woosah

SELF-WORTH IS NET-WORTH

ON THE MENU

We have all heard the phrase "bring something to the table" or "having a seat at the table," but have you ever considered coming empty-handed or bypassing a seat altogether? Maybe, just maybe, you are on the menu, the entrée, or you are the table.

In other words, what if others needed to bring something to or glean something from you? This is how you must see yourself.

I'm talking about having confidence in what you bring, your skills, and your capabilities.

By default, your essence is diversified, not just because you're a woman of color but also because there is only one of you. You are emphatically like no other, which is the epitome of diversity. Sis, you must show up as the authentic you every day!

When you aren't your authentic self, the company loses an opportunity to learn from you—i.e., your perspective and ideas. Your background has led you to this point, and because of it, you have profound knowledge, a new approach, and fresh strategies. Why suppress this?

Think about it: diverse companies are better equipped to appeal to talented job candidates because they respect, reflect, and celebrate different ideas, perspectives, and backgrounds. Being yourself helps to support this.

SELF-WORTH

So, despite the disheartening stats and uneven playing field (expounded in chapter 3), take a moment to reflect on everything that has led you to this point in your career. Think about the hardships, long hours, and even longer nights, sacrifices, successes, failures, and adversities.

The good news is that you are here right now, so that means you got through them. You can process and reflect on what you learned in Woosah's chapter 3. In other words, whatever hardships you are currently going through will eventually become a distant memory of reflection as well.

Let me ask you this: If you could go back ten years, what advice would you give yourself?

WHAT ADVICE WOULD I GIVE MYSELF FROM 10 YRS AGO?

- ☐ _____
- ☐ _____
- ☐ _____

Guess what? You can use the same advice you would have given yourself ten years ago, now! Believe it or not, it is still applicable even after all this time. Understand that nothing lasts forever. That said, you will persist through hard times!

Every obstacle is an opportunity to be groomed into who and what we're supposed to be, even when it's painfully harsh and especially tough. Barriers provide us with tools for our tool kits—tools that we would not have if we hadn't struggled at some point in time.

WHAT ARE SOME OF YOUR TOP STRENGTHS?
(Think of work examples where you naturally demonstrated these)

- ☐ _____
- ☐ _____
- ☐ _____

YOU ARE ON THE MENU

Stop fighting for a seat at the table. You are on the menu, sis, so serve a side of you.

WHAT ARE YOU SERVING?

(i.e., your "uniqueness" and what sets you apart from other colleagues)

_____
_____
_____
_____
_____
_____
_____

WHAT DO YOU LOVE ABOUT YOURSELF?

_____
_____
_____

Now, I want you to study, embrace, and own everything you listed above. Practice saying your answers aloud. Be confident and sell yourself! Highlight your strengths and skills, and believe that the diversity you bring to the table is incomparable.

UPROOTING INAUTHENTICITY

Addressing an issue's root helps provide insight and reduces the likelihood of resurfacing.

WHAT IS KEEPING ME FROM BEING MORE AUTHENTIC IN THE WORKPLACE?

_____

_____

_____

WHAT IS THE ROOT OF THIS?

⬇

AND WHAT DOES THIS DO TO YOU?

⬇

AND WHAT DOES THIS DO FOR YOU?

⬇

SO, WHY DOES THIS MATTER?

⬇

SO, WHAT ARE YOU GOING TO DO ABOUT IT?

AFFIRMATION

THE AUTHENTIC ME IS NEEDED IN THE WORKPLACE AND EVERY SPACE I ENTER.

GOD INTENTIONALLY GIFTED ME WITH THIS PERSONALITY, UNIQUENESS, AND ESSENCE.

I WILL NO LONGER SUPPRESS THIS.

YOU ARE ON THE MENU

Stop fighting for a seat at the table. You are on the menu, sis, so serve a side of you.

IN WHAT WAYS CAN YOU BE MORE AUTHENTIC IN AND OUT OF THE WORKPLACE?

_____
_____
_____
_____
_____
_____

HOW CAN YOU LEVERAGE AND DISPLAY YOUR UNIQUE SKILLS/GIFTS MORE INTENTIONALLY IN THE WORKPLACE?

_____
_____
_____
_____
_____
_____

ON THE MENU

SELF-WORTH IS NET WORTH

Jot down 2-3 affirmations that will encourage a more authentic you. Say them before starting your work day. Practice gratitude as well!

DAILY AFFIRMATIONS

_____
_____
_____
_____

I AM MOST GRATEFUL FOR

_____
_____
_____
_____

TODAY'S SELF-CARE GOALS

_____
_____
_____
_____

Sis, you are definitely on the menu and are at the table, so let them take a seat and experience a side of you that they've never tasted.

SPEAK, SIS. SPEAK!
notes

SPEAK, SIS. SPEAK!

notes

SPEAK, SIS. SPEAK!

notes

> **WHERE I AM IN LIFE IS INDICATIVE OF THE WORK THAT I HAVE OR HAVEN'T PUT IN.**
>
> —RAHKAL SHELTON ROBERSON

7 KEYS TO OBTAINING A MORE FULFILLING WORK EXPERIENCE

KNOW THAT YOU ARE A THERMOSTAT, NOT A THERMOMETER

KEY #4

KNOWING HOW TO NAVIGATE TOXIC WORK ENVIRONMENTS, MANAGE STRESS, AND SET BOUNDARIES IS ESSENTIAL TO YOUR PEACE.

Lessons for Chapters 4-6 in Woosah

TOXIC ENVIRONMENTS + STRESS MANAGEMENT + SETTING BOUNDARIES

NAVIGATING WITH GRACE

We all know what it's like to work in stressful situations and environments that are not conducive to our livelihoods, health, and personal goals we've set for ourselves. We also understand that stress kills literally and figuratively. Chapters 4-6 in Woosah: A Survival Guide for Women of Color Working In Corporate address toxic environments, managing stress, and boundary setting. Read those chapters to maximize the activities in this section better.

First, I want you to know that there is a difference between work stress and toxic environments. A toxic environment is so much bigger than just having a bad (stress-filled) day or being displeased with coming to work. Toxic environments are environments that impact your health (mentally, physically, or emotionally). The negativity is ongoing and a part of that workplace's culture.

Second, the work atmosphere/culture and environment usually force great workers to quit, elevate their blood pressure and drive them to happy hours or hour-long sessions on therapy couches.

In contrast, work stress can be triggered by deadlines, workloads, and a lack of support on a project or task. See the difference?

Feeling bouts of stress in our jobs is normal. However, toxic environments harm our health and personal and professional growth.

Are you working in a toxic environment? How do you navigate work adversities with grace?

Let's identify what a toxic environment looks like:

How happy are you with your current workplace?

EMPLOYMENT SATISFACTION

Can you focus on learning what you can (while you're there) and use this info as a stepping stone or launch pad for your next move?

8 SIGNS YOU WORK IN A TOXIC ENVIRONMENT

Pg 69 in Woosah provides in-depth examples

CLIQUES, DISCRIMINATION, PRIVILEGE, NEPOTISM, & FAVORITISM

INEFFECTIVE LEADERSHIP & MANAGEMENT

CONNIVING BEHAVIORS & TOXIC PEOPLE

OPPRESSIVE GOSSIP CULTURES

SILOS & HESITANT COLLABORATIONS

PRODUCES NEGATIVE HEALTH CHANGES

POOR COMMUNICATION & HIGH TURNOVER

LITTLE TO NO ROOM FOR GROWTH

WHAT TOXICITY COULD LOOK LIKE

BAD LEADERSHIP

MICROMANAGING

GASLIGHTING

LACK OF BOUNDARIES

INNAPPROPRIATE REQUEST & BEHAVIORS

LACK OF ACCOUNTABILITY

CONIVING BEHAVIORS

THROWING UNDER THE BUS

STEALING IDEAS, DISTRUSTING ENVIRONMENT

LAZINESS, NOT PULLING WEIGHT

GOSSIPING & SLANDER

UNNECESSARY CC'ING, REPORTING & KAREN BEHAVIORS

CLIQUES + DISCRIMINATION

HAVING YOUR JUDGMENT CONSTANTLY QUESTIONS

BULLIES & MEANGIRLS

PERKS ONLY OFFERED TO CERTAIN PEOPLE

LACK OF COLLOBRATION & SILOS

LACK OF PROMOTION FOR WOC

HEALTH CHANGES

ANXIETY & HEART PALPS

FEAR OF LOSING JOB OR DROPPING THE BALL

DEPRESSION

STRESSED & BURNOUT

FEELINGS OF DISTRUST AND UNPROTECTED

ACTIVITY TIME

WHAT IS YOUR MANAGER'S STYLE LIKE? DOES IT WORK FOR YOU?

_____
_____
_____
_____
_____
_____
_____

WHAT ARE THREE THINGS YOU WISH YOUR MANAGER DID, DID MORE OF OR BETTER?

01 _____

02 _____

03 _____

Does your job invite feedback or assessment forms for manager evaluations? This may be good content for your next one-on-one, if communicated tactfully.

> **CULTURE IS MORE IMPORTANT THAN SIMPLY A VISION.**
>
> **SOME LEADERS HAVE GREAT VISION BUT HAVE CREATED A TOXIC CULTURE WHERE THAT VISION WILL NEVER HAPPEN.**
>
> —PHIL COOKE

KARENS IN THE WORKPLACE

Karen and Kevin's personas are highly infiltrated in the workplace, especially in corporate cultures.

They aren't just single people but a cross between white privilege, entitlement, self-appointed policing, and simply harassing behaviors. This persona is demanding beyond the scope of what's necessary and/or reasonable at the expense of others, specifically Black people.

They are often decision-makers and relentlessly try to tear down and minimize Black and Brown people to make themselves feel good.

People like this conspire to trip others up and get them reprimanded, written up, or even fired. As self-appointed watchdogs, they wait for trouble and then pounce on it.

-Chapter Four
Woosah: A Survival Guide for Women of Color Working In Corporate

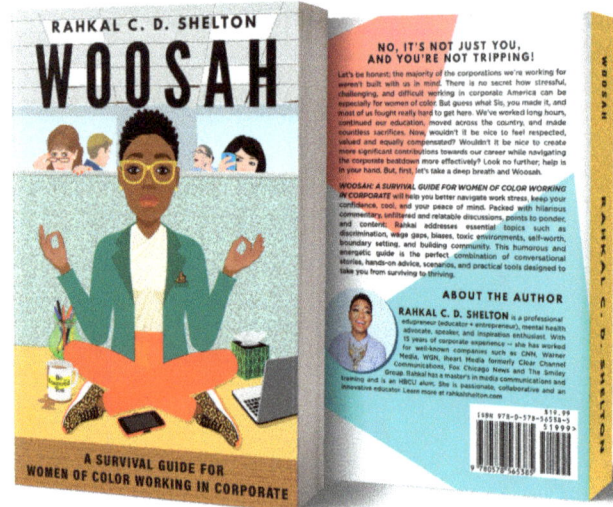

HAVE YOU OBSERVED TOXIC BEHAVIORS/PEOPLE IN YOUR WORKPLACE? IF SO, WRITE IT DOWN.

_____
_____
_____
_____

These are the people/behaviors you want to avoid whenever possible; keep boundaries between them and you. Limit your conversations to the business at hand. You can use the back of your journal for additional writing space.

ARE THERE ANY KARENS OR KEVINS IN YOUR WORKPLACE? HOW HAVE OR HOW WOULD YOU HANDLE THEIR BEHAVIORS?

_____
_____
_____

WHAT TYPE OF WORK ENVIRONMENT DO YOU THRIVE IN?

_____
_____

HAS WORK IMPACTED YOUR HEALTH, LATELY (GOOD OR BAD)?

_____
_____

Use the back of your journal for additional writing space.

WHEN ARE YOU MOST EXCITED, FEELING VALUED, AND LIKE YOU'RE MAKING CONTRIBUTIONS?

_____
_____
_____
_____

HOW DO YOU LIKE TO BE MANAGED? HAVE YOU EVER NEEDED TO MANAGE UP (MAKING YOUR BOSS'S JOB EASIER BY MANAGING YOUR MANAGER)?

_____
_____
_____
_____
_____

WHEN WAS THE LAST TIME YOU'VE EXPERIENCED WORK-RELATED ANXIETY OR STRESS? WHAT TRIGGERED THIS?

_____
_____
_____

WHAT ARE YOUR STRESS COPING MECHANISMS? HOW DO YOU DE-STRESS AT WORK?

_____
_____
_____
_____
_____
_____

IF YOUR ENVIRONMENT NEGATIVELY IMPACTS YOUR HEALTH, IT MAY BE TIME TO FIRE YOUR EMPLOYER. LIST THE PROS AND CONS OF STAYING WHERE YOU ARE.

_____
_____
_____
_____
_____
_____
_____
_____
_____

NAVIGATING WITH GRACE
ACTION PLAN

MICHELLE OBAMA
KILL THEM WITH KINDNESS. WHEN THEY GO LOW, WE GO HIGH!

DECIDE
IS THIS ENVIRONMENT RIGHT FOR YOU?

SET BOUNDARIES
SET BOUNDARIES AND CLARIFY WHAT YOU WILL AND WILL NOT ENGAGE IN, ALLOW, OR TOLERATE.

STUDY POLICY AND DOCUMENT EVERYTHING
MORE SPECIFICALLY, DOCUMENT INAPPROPRIATE INCIDENTS, BEHAVIORS, AND POLICY CONFLICTS. KEEP THIS FOR YOUR RECORDS.

IDENTIFY WHO IS IN CHARGE
PLEASE KNOW WHO YOUR HR REPS ARE AND WHO REPORTS TO WHOM. UNDERSTAND THE ORGANIZATIONAL CHARTS AND CHAIN OF COMMAND IN CASE YOU NEED THIS INFO.

SELF-CARE
YOU CAN EXERCISE SELF-CARE ON THE JOB BY SETTING BOUNDARIES, WATCHING YOUR FAVORITE SHOW, OR TAKING A NAP IN YOUR CAR DURING LUNCH BREAKS. TAKE A STROLL AROUND THE BUILDING, TAKE BREAKS WHEN NEEDED, WORK REMOTELY OR CONNECT WITH YOUR WORK TRIBE.

FOR MORE ON TOXIC ENVIRONMENT ACTION PLANS, READ CHAPTER FOUR OF WOOSAH: A SURVIVAL GUIDE FOR WOMEN OF COLOR WORKING IN CORPORATE

ACTIVITY TIME

LIST WHAT YOU CURRENTLY DISLIKE ABOUT YOUR DUTIES AND/OR WORKPLACE.

_____
_____
_____
_____
_____
_____

HOW DO THE DISPLEASURES ABOVE MAKE YOU FEEL (PHYSICALLY AND EMOTIONALLY)?

_____
_____
_____

WHAT CAN YOU DO ABOUT IT?

_____
_____
_____

IF YOU ARE LESS STRESSED AT WORK, THERE WILL BE A LOWER CHANCE OF THE STRESS FOLLOWING YOU HOME. AND IF YOU HAVE LESS STRESS AT HOME, YOU'LL HAVE A BETTER CHANCE OF NOT BRINGING STRESS TO WORK.

SO, WHAT CAN YOU DO? CHANGE COURSES WHEN YOU FEEL YOUR STRESS LEVELS RISING. WORK TO REDUCE STRESS FROM YOUR PERSONAL AND PROFESSIONAL LIFE.

HAVE A STRATEGY IN PLACE, AND REFRAIN FROM TRANSFERRING STRESS.

-CHAPTER FIVE
WOOSAH: A SURVIVAL GUIDE FOR WOMEN OF COLOR WORKING IN CORPORATE

REALISTIC CAPACITY

Sometimes eliminating stress at work will require you to be open and honest with yourself. Knowing your limitations and the seasons you're currently in better equips you with understanding what you have to give.

Each season will look different.

WHAT IS YOUR JOB REQUIRING OF YOU?

LIST ALL NEW OR UNREALISTIC DEMANDS

_____

_____

_____

WHAT IS YOUR CURRENT CAPACITY?

WHAT ARE WILLING AND ABLE TO GIVE?

_____

_____

_____

WHAT ARE THE PROS OF YOUR CURRENT JOB?

_____

_____

_____

WHAT ARE THE CONS OF YOUR CURRENT JOB?

_____

_____

_____

> **BE SURE TO GET CLEAR EXPECTATIONS OF WHAT'S REQUIRED AND EXPECTED OF YOU (IN WRITING) BEFORE ACCEPTING ANY POSITION.**
>
> **AND SHARE YOUR EXPECTATIONS AND NEEDS, TOO!**
>
> **–RAHKAL SHELTON ROBERSON**

WORK STRESS TRIGGERS

- **LOW WAGES & BEING UNDERPAID**
- **LITTLE TO NO ACKNOWLEDGMENT**
- **LACK OF WORK-LIFE BALANCE**
- **HEAVY WORKLOADS**
- **GASLIGHTING, MICROAGGRESSIONS, DISCRIMINATION & BIASES**
- **IMPOSSIBLE EXPECTATIONS**
- **PLAYING A ROLE SELF (WEARING A MASK)**
- **LITTLE TO NO ROOM FOR GROWTH**
- **MINIMAL PROFESSIONAL DEVELOPMENT OPPORTUNITIES**

RACIAL MICROAGGRESSIVE TRIGGERS

- **WOW, YOU'RE SO ARTICULATE** (as if surprised that you can speak)
- **ACCUSATIONS OF BEING AGGRESSIVE** (when speaking confidently)
- **STEREOTYPICAL ASSUMPTIONS ABOUT YOUR UPBRINGING, LIFESTYLE, IDEALS, ETC.** (usually revealed in conversation)
- **INAPPROPRIATE HAIR QUESTIONS AND REACHING TO TOUCH IT** (this one is classic and beyond flagrant)
- **NARRATIVES CREATED FOR YOU** (putting unauthorized words in your mouth)
- **COMMENTS LIKE "YOU'RE ONE OF THE GOOD ONES," OR USING WEIRD SLANGS ONLY WHEN TALKING TO YOU**
  (monitor if this dialect or word choice only changes around you or other POC)

WOOSAH GUIDE
MANAGING LIFE AND WORK STRESS

Because stress is inevitable, the best thing we can do is to reduce it as much as possible. Identifying triggers and putting a plan in place is golden. Below are a couple of suggestions.

GET ORGANIZED & PRIORITIZE
Get organized. Prioritize your time with a to-do list. Leave a little flex room if something urgent arises and you're thrown off course.

SAY NO!
Say no and mean it. If it is completely out of your job description or it will conflict with something of a higher priority and significance, say no. If it leads to a hefty dose of stress, say no.

LET IT RING!
Do not answer! Send the person to voicemail. You don't always have to respond to calls, texts, or notifications.

TABLE IT
Can it wait until tomorrow? Is it important or urgent? You know there is a difference between these two situations. Important means the task must be completed. Urgent means the task requires an immediate response.

LAST CALL
Manage your time wisely and set a cut-off time.

HEY BEAUTIFUL. HOW ARE YOU FEELING? WE'RE HALFWAY DONE, AND YOU'RE DOING FABULOUS!

REMEMBER YOU HAVE EXTRA PAGES IN THE BACK IF YOU NEED MORE WRITING SPACE☺.

ALSO, AS WE UNPACKED STRESS MANAGEMENT AND ENTER INTO THE BOUNDARY DISCUSSION, HERE'S SOMETHING TO CONSIDER.

You'll have to let go of caring what people will think after you push back or prioritize your well-being. As long as you're tasteful, thoughtful, and respectful in your delivery, how they perceive it is their problem.

BOUNDARIES
VULNERABLE AREAS

Sometimes, we don't have words for our feelings; we just know we aren't good, burned out, anxious, or stressed. First things first, let's identify where you need boundaries. Think through your vulnerable areas that need protecting. See examples below and think about your life.

WORKING RANDOM AFTER-HOURS INSTEAD OF PRIORITIZING PERSONAL TIME

BEING CURSED/YELLED AT OR INTIMIDATED IN THE WORKPLACE

COLLEAGUES TOUCHING YOUR HAIR, TOUCHING YOU, OR INVADING YOUR PERSONAL SPACE

BOSSES THREATENING TO FIRE YOU OR WITHHOLD INCOME/BONUS ETC

YOUR BOSS OR TEAM REACHING OUT AFTER HOURS OR EXPECTING YOU TO ALWAYS BE AVAILABLE

BEING ASKED TO DO CONSTANT FAVORS

YOUR COWORKER CONSTANTLY DUMPING THEIR DRAMA OR RELATIONSHIP PROBLEMS ON YOU

YOUR BOSS ASKING ABOUT PERSONAL DETAILS OF YOUR WEEKEND AND PERSONAL LIFE

Lessons for Chapter 6 in Woosah

SAMPLE TALKING POINTS

BOUNDARIES IN THE WORKPLACE

"I CAN ONLY MEET FOR 30 MINS."

"I CAN'T HAVE THIS CONVERSATION HERE. IT ISN'T APPROPRIATE FOR WORK."

"IF YOU'RE GOING TO BE LATE, PLEASE LET ME KNOW AHEAD OF TIME, SO I CAN PLAN ACCORDINGLY."

"HEY, WE SEE THINGS DIFFERENTLY, AND THAT'S FINE. I RESPECT YOUR OPINION, BUT PLEASE DON'T FORCE IT ON ME."

"I WOULD APPRECIATE IT IF YOU TALKED TO ME IN A RESPECTFUL TONE."

"IT MAKES ME UNCOMFORTABLE WHEN YOU TOUCH ME OR INVADE MY PERSONAL SPACE. IF YOU CAN'T RESPECT MY SPACE, I CAN'T WORK WITH YOU."

"I UNDERSTAND YOU HAVE A LOT GOING ON, AND I WANT TO BE HERE FOR YOU, BUT I HAVE A LOT GOING ON, TOO, AND I JUST DON'T HAVE THE CAPACITY FOR BOTH OF US."

"PLEASE DON'T CONTACT ME AFTER WORKING HOURS. IT IMPEDES MY PERSONAL TIME."

"ANY WORK THAT DIDN'T GET FINISHED TODAY WILL BE PRIORITIZED TOMORROW."

BOUNDARY SETTING
ACTION PLAN

STEP ONE

IDENTIFY YOUR AREAS OF VULNERABILITY AND WHERE BOUNDARIES ARE NEEDED IN YOUR LIFE (PERSONALLY AND PROFESSIONALLY).

STEP TWO

CREATE TALKING POINTS OF WHAT YOU CAN SAY WHEN YOUR BOUNDARIES ARE COMPROMISED.

STEP THREE

SAY YOUR TALKING POINTS. STICK TO THE PLAN AND MEAN WHAT YOU SAY!

ACTIVITY TIME

WHAT CAUSES DISCOMFORT, ANNOYANCE, EMOTIONAL DRAIN, OR PAIN IN THE WORKPLACE?

_____
_____
_____
_____
_____
_____
_____
_____
_____
_____
_____
_____
_____
_____
_____
_____
_____
_____

BENEFITS OF
BOUNDARY SETTING

- ENCOURAGES RESPECT (FOR YOURSELF) AND FROM OTHERS

- REDUCES STRESS AND BURNOUT

- IMPROVES EMOTIONAL AND MENTAL HEALTH

- SUPPORTS MORE REWARDING AND SUSTAINABLE RELATIONSHIPS

- HELPS PROVIDE CLEAR EXPECTATIONS

- REDUCES OBLIGATORY ACTIONS

ACTIVITY TIME

JOT DOWN 2-3 BOUNDARIES YOU CAN SET FOR YOURSELF IN THE WORKPLACE, PERSONALLY, OR WHEN WORKING WITH CLIENTS. THESE WILL HELP FOSTER A MORE PEACEFUL EXPERIENCE.

TIME BOUNDARY

_____
_____
_____
_____

PHYSICAL BOUNDARY

_____
_____
_____
_____

EMOTIONAL (PEACE PROTECTION)

_____
_____
_____
_____

SOCIAL BOUNDARY

_____
_____
_____
_____

MORAL + ETHICS

_____
_____
_____

SPEAK, SIS. SPEAK!

notes

SPEAK, SIS. SPEAK!
notes

SPEAK, SIS. SPEAK!

notes

> **LEADERSHIP IS NOT A POSITION; IT'S A POSTURE.**
>
> —UNKNOWN

7 KEYS TO OBTAINING A MORE FULFILLING WORK EXPERIENCE

KNOW THAT HAVING A SOLID COMMUNITY AND TRIBE IS GOLDEN

KEY #5

IF YOU WANT TO GO FAST, GO ALONE; IF YOU WANT TO GO FAR, GO TOGETHER.
            -AFRICAN PROVERB

> Read Chapter 7 in Woosah

COMMUNITIES, TRIBES & NETWORKING

TRIBES

Sis, there are no islands, and everyone got to where they are in their careers, work, and life with S-U-P-P-O-R-T! Don't let anyone tell you differently. We all need someone, and we are all connected to people in one way or another. Therefore, I do not believe in the phrase "self-made." Granted, many of us have done the heavy lifting at times with little to no support, and many of us feel we are the ones making things happen. I get it.

But I genuinely believe it is the Lord orchestrating the strings, contacts, contracts, encounters, opportunities, and connections in our lives. Whether you're a believer or not, you didn't get to where you are on your own.

Behind every successful woman of color is a story filled with a tribe of others supporting, rooting for, and cheering her on. Maybe these tribes were invisible and not in the forefront, but they were present in your journey at critical times and places.

Maybe it was that stranger who paid you a compliment on a difficult day or that college counselor who helped you straighten out your financial aid situation. Perhaps it was that teacher who believed in you, the other woman of color on the interview panel, who advocated for you behind closed doors and helped you get the job. Whomever these Godsends were, they were there to help you along the way. They were a part of your tribe.

Tribes and communities are critical to maintaining sanity, peace, and success. And we all need them. You'll need to network and build genuine mutual relationships for tremendous success.

NETWORKING
WHAT IT AIN'T

Networking is not what others can do for you. It is not a "what you can get and how you can benefit" mentality.

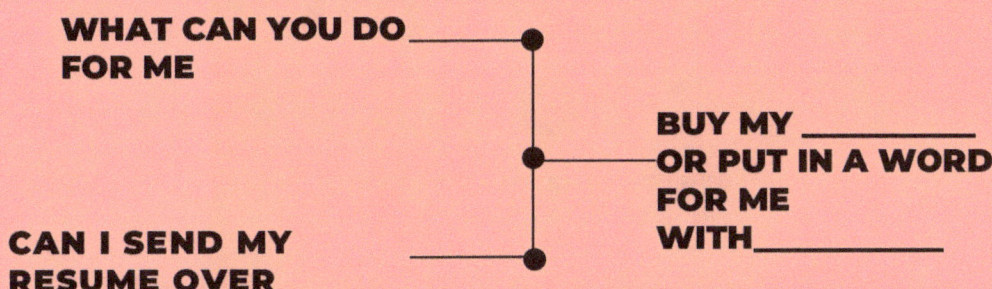

- WHAT CAN YOU DO FOR ME
- CAN I SEND MY RESUME OVER
- BUY MY _____ OR PUT IN A WORD FOR ME WITH _____

NETWORKING
WHAT IT IS

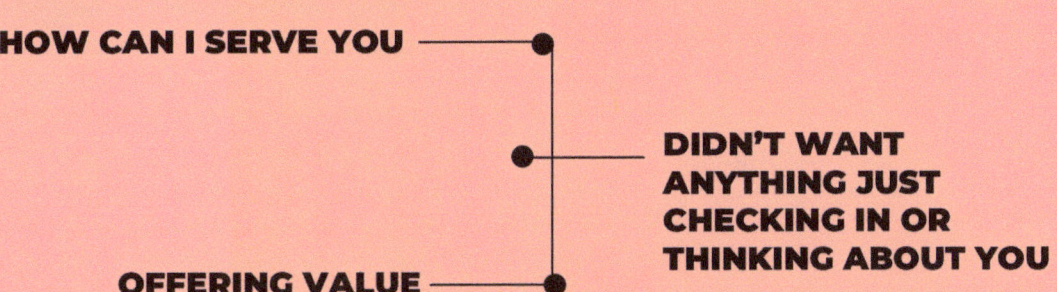

- HOW CAN I SERVE YOU
- OFFERING VALUE
- DIDN'T WANT ANYTHING JUST CHECKING IN OR THINKING ABOUT YOU

No, I am not suggesting that you be the only one doing the giving; instead, switch your mind to giving vs. receiving. The more you give and serve, the more you will get back in return. Doing this lays a strong foundation and provides a more natural way of connecting with individuals to build your community. It also displays your value.

IT'S ESSENTIAL FOR WOC TO HAVE A TRUSTED ADVOCATE IN THE WORKPLACE.

Ideally, this person is more seasoned, and influential and can provide coaching and support for your workplace needs. You've made this connection by properly networking. And, sis, while you're looking for an advocate, be one for someone else.

STRATEGIES FOR COMMUNITY BUILDING

It can be challenging to foster genuine connections in this instant-digital age that we're in, but putting in the effort can breed many rewards. I believe there is a tribe for everyone, and they are essential. I'm not talking about transactional relationships either but those welcoming of vulnerability.

BE INTENTIONAL WITH POSITIONING AND EFFORTS BUT ALSO ORGANIC IN THE APPROACH
If it's a vibe you'll know and feel it.

BE CONSISTENT AND SELECTIVE
I do not suggest stretching yourself thin or putting yourself in obligatory situations. Pick a few to connect with and be intentional about those.

JOIN AFFINITY/BUSINESS RESOURCE GROUPS OR ALUM ASSOCIATIONS
This is a great space to meet other professionals.

SPEAK, SMILE AND BE INVITING
Your demeanor and energy say it all. Be what you would want to attract in your community.

ENGAGE ON SOCIAL MEDIA/LINKEDIN WITH OTHER PROFESSIONALS IN YOUR INDUSTRY
Even if they don't follow you, if you're interested in the content... please feel free to engage with it.

VOLUNTEER
Manage your time wisely and set a cut-off time.

> TWO ARE BETTER THAN ONE BECAUSE THEY HAVE A GOOD RETURN FOR THEIR LABOR: IF EITHER OF THEM FALLS DOWN, ONE CAN HELP THE OTHER UP.
>
> BUT PITY ANYONE WHO FALLS AND HAS NO ONE TO HELP THEM UP.
>
> -ECCLESIASTES 4:9-10

ACTIVITY TIME

LIST A FEW QUALITIES YOU'D LIKE TO SEE IN THE PEOPLE YOU WOULD LIKE TO SURROUND YOURSELF WITH.

_____

_____

_____

_____

(Are you demonstrating these same qualities?)

IDENTIFY 2-3 PEOPLE YOU ADMIRE (FROM YOUR COMPANY OR A SPECIFIC DEPARTMENT, ALUM ASSOCIATION, AFFINITY GROUP, CLASS, CHURCH, OR WHEREVER), ASK THEM FOR COFFEE OR TEA, AND LEARN THEIR STORIES.

_____

_____

_____

_____

Keep in touch with the people listed above. Create calendar reminders to check in with them. Invite them to places, and ask to support them. Nurture these growing relationships!

ACTIVITY TIME

IDENTIFY 1-2 NETWORKING EVENTS OR PROFESSIONAL DEVELOPMENT OPPORTUNITIES, REACH OUT TO THE ORGANIZER AND ASK HOW YOU CAN SUPPORT THEM.

_____
_____
_____
_____

PRACTICE BEING, DOING, AND GIVING WHAT YOU WOULD LIKE TO RECEIVE FROM YOUR COMMUNITY.

_____
_____
_____
_____

Ensure your LinkedIn profile is updated, appropriate, and adequately depicts your skills. Connect with people there.

SPEAK, SIS. SPEAK!

notes

SPEAK, SIS. SPEAK!
notes

SPEAK, SIS. SPEAK!

notes

7 KEYS TO OBTAINING A MORE FULFILLING WORK EXPERIENCE

KNOW THAT WITHOUT A VISION, PLAN OR DISCIPLINE, YOU CAN'T GO FAR

KEY #6

YOU DO NOT RISE TO THE LEVEL OF YOUR GOALS. YOU FALL TO THE LEVEL OF YOUR SYSTEMS.   -JAMES CLEAR

Lessons for Chapter 8 in Woosah

GOALDIGGER

Hey lady, I know you want to do more than survive. I want you to, as well. As a matter of fact, I hope that you'll thrive in every workplace.

I would love to see you succeed in corporate (public and private sectors), nonprofit, entrepreneurship, relationships, and all areas of your career and life.

As a certified professional coach, workplace peace advocate, and champion for women, the one thing I found most effective is writing our goals and plans down, having accountability, crazy faith, discipline, and an action plan to make it happen. Did I say discipline already? Discipline is the key to success, but you can't do it solo. You truly need some accountability!

I want to close our time with strategic goal-setting and planning materials to ensure you're equipped with the tools to obtain a more fulfilling work experience. Think of 1-2 people you can work through this workbook with or who can keep you accountable.

Now, if you've decided you've had enough of your workplace after doing these activities, I have something for you too. I've also included a couple of job-hunting and career resources.

You can use this same material in the entrepreneurial world and for some of your personal goals.

Whatever you do, make the most of this. Be sure to get really clear and specific about where you'd like to be.

WHAT CHA' WORKING WITH
TALENT ASSESMENT

I previously mentioned that everyone was created with unique giftings and talents. Our gifts are innate; we were born with these and excel in these areas naturally. We all have them, which proves we're all good at something!

Skills are the areas of our expertise, which are things we accumulate. Skills are learned and developed; they are not our gifts! Our gifts aligned with purpose.

Many times we try to achieve success in areas that we are only skilled in but need to be gifted for. Talents are what we're good at, while our gifts are God-given.

Therefore, God gives provision in our areas of giftings vs. talents because our purpose is usually tied to our gifts. I hope this makes sense.

However, all three (skills, talents, and gifts) can work together to support our success when we appropriate them accordingly. Let's take inventory of what we're working with.

MY GIFTINGS ARE:

_____
_____
_____
_____

MY TALENTS ARE:

_____
_____
_____
_____

I AM SKILLED AT:

_____
_____
_____
_____

WHAT ARE SOME WAYS I CAN LEVERAGE ALL THREE?

_____

_____

_____

SPEAK, SIS. SPEAK!
notes

_____
_____
_____
_____
_____
_____
_____
_____
_____
_____
_____

SUCCESS
ACTION PLAN

STEP ONE

PRAY FOR CLARITY AND ASK GOD TO REVEAL YOUR PURPOSE. IF YOU ALREADY KNOW IT, BE INTENTIONAL ABOUT TAKING AND MAKING DAILY OPPORTUNITIES THAT ALIGN WITH IT.

STEP TWO

NURTURE AND SHARPEN YOUR TALENTS, SKILLS, AND GIFTS BY TAKING COURSES, ATTENDING WORKSHOPS, READING BOOKS, AND DOING PURPOSED-ALIGNED ACTIVITIES.

STEP THREE

MAKE A LIST OF 2-3 OPPORTUNITIES YOU CAN APPLY FOR OR LOOK FOR WAYS TO CREATE YOUR OWN OPPORTUNITIES THAT ARE PURPOSE ALIGNED.

SMART GOALS

Create 2-3 professional goals that you want to accomplish that align with your purpose, gifts, and dreams.

When setting goals, make sure it follows the SMART structure. Use the questions below to create your goals.

S	**SPECIFIC** WHAT DO I WANT TO ACCOMPLISH THIS YEAR?	
M	**MEASURABLE** HOW WILL I KNOW WHEN IT IS ACCOMPLISHED?	
A	**ACHIEVABLE** HOW CAN THE GOAL BE ACCOMPLISHED?	
R	**RELEVANT** DOES THIS ALIGN WITH MY PURPOSE AND DREAMS?	
T	**TIME BOUND** WHEN CAN I ACCOMPLISH THIS GOAL?	

HOLISTIC YOU

While we're predominately addressing the workplace and our professional aspirations, our personal lives must also be accounted for. You can't thrive professionally if you're no good privately. Our personhood and mindsets are the drivers of our lives. Moreover, if you do achieve professional success while your personal life is in shambles, it won't last. So, sis, let's look at our personal lives, too.

For each category below, write down things you are doing well and where you need improvement. Take the time to reflect on these, and write a goal for each category.

CATEGORY	WHAT I'M DOING WELL	WHERE I NEED IMPROVEMENT	MY GOALS
FAMILY			
FRIENDS			
WORK/SCHOOL			
BODY			
MENTAL HEALTH			
SPIRITUALITY			

> **YOU DO NOT RISE TO THE LEVEL OF YOUR GOALS. YOU FALL TO THE LEVEL OF YOUR SYSTEMS.**
>
> —JAMES CLEAR

MONTHLY GOALS
TRACKER

James Clear so eloquently encourages us to create healthy habits and systems that will support the success of our goals. He says, "You do not rise to the level of your goals. You fall to the level of your systems."

A goal without an actual plan or system is just a wish. So, please take a moment and create your actual system to make sure these goals are met. Let's think through it from a monthly perspective first.

	MY GOALS	1-2 THINGS I WILL DO TO ENSURE IT GETS DONE	DONE
JANUARY			○
FEBUARY			○
MARCH			○
APRIL			○
MAY			○
JUNE			○

MONTHLY GOALS
(EXTRA SPACE)

MONTHLY GOALS
TRACKER

James Clear so eloquently encourages us to create healthy habits and systems that will support the success of our goals. He says, "You do not rise to the level of your goals. You fall to the level of your systems."

A goal without an actual plan or system is just a wish. So, please take a moment and create your actual system to make sure these goals are met. Let's think through it from a monthly perspective first.

	MY GOALS	1-2 THINGS I WILL DO TO ENSURE IT GETS DONE	DONE
JULY			○
AUG			○
SEPT			○
OCT			○
NOV			○
DEC			○

MONTHLY GOALS
(EXTRA SPACE)

WEEKLY GOAL TRACKER

Now let's break our monthly goals down into weekly goals! Breaking them down is a great way to reduce feeling overwhelmed. The smaller task also helps to ensure the goals are specific, measurable, relative, and timely.

Ps. there is one month's worth of weekly sheets added to this workbook, but you can use your blank journal pages to document subsequent weeks each month.

WEEK #: _____

	JAN'S GOALS	1-2 THINGS I WILL DO TO ENSURE IT GETS DONE	DONE
MON			○
TUE			○
WED			○
THU			○
FRI			○
SAT			○
SUN			○

WEEKLY GOAL TRACKER

Now let's break our monthly goals down into weekly goals! Breaking them down is a great way to reduce feeling overwhelmed. The smaller task also helps to ensure the goals are specific, measurable, relative, and timely.

Ps. there is one month's worth of weekly sheets added to this workbook, but you can use your blank journal pages to document subsequent weeks each month.

WEEK #: _____

	JAN'S GOALS	1-2 THINGS I WILL DO TO ENSURE IT GETS DONE	DONE
MON			○
TUE			○
WED			○
THU			○
FRI			○
SAT			○
SUN			○

WEEKLY GOAL TRACKER

Now let's break our monthly goals down into weekly goals! Breaking them down is a great way to reduce feeling overwhelmed. The smaller task also helps to ensure the goals are specific, measurable, relative, and timely.

Ps. there is one month's worth of weekly sheets added to this workbook, but you can use your blank journal pages to document subsequent weeks each month.

WEEK #: _____

	JAN'S GOALS	1-2 THINGS I WILL DO TO ENSURE IT GETS DONE	DONE
MON			○
TUE			○
WED			○
THU			○
FRI			○
SAT			○
SUN			○

WEEKLY GOAL TRACKER

Now let's break our monthly goals down into weekly goals! Breaking them down is a great way to reduce feeling overwhelmed. The smaller task also helps to ensure the goals are specific, measurable, relative, and timely.

Ps. there is one month's worth of weekly sheets added to this workbook, but you can use your blank journal pages to document subsequent weeks each month.

WEEK #: _____

	JAN'S GOALS	1-2 THINGS I WILL DO TO ENSURE IT GETS DONE	DONE
MON			○
TUE			○
WED			○
THU			○
FRI			○
SAT			○
SUN			○

DAILY CHECKLIST

List out a couple of daily tasks that you can do to ensure you're inching towards your goals.

- [ ] _____
- [ ] _____
- [ ] _____
- [ ] _____
- [ ] _____
- [ ] _____

GOALS ON PURPOSE

Achieving our goals depends on whether our systems are effective and if we are taking action. Where we are in life reflects the work we have or haven't put in.

Use the table below to understand the "why" of your goals.

GOAL:

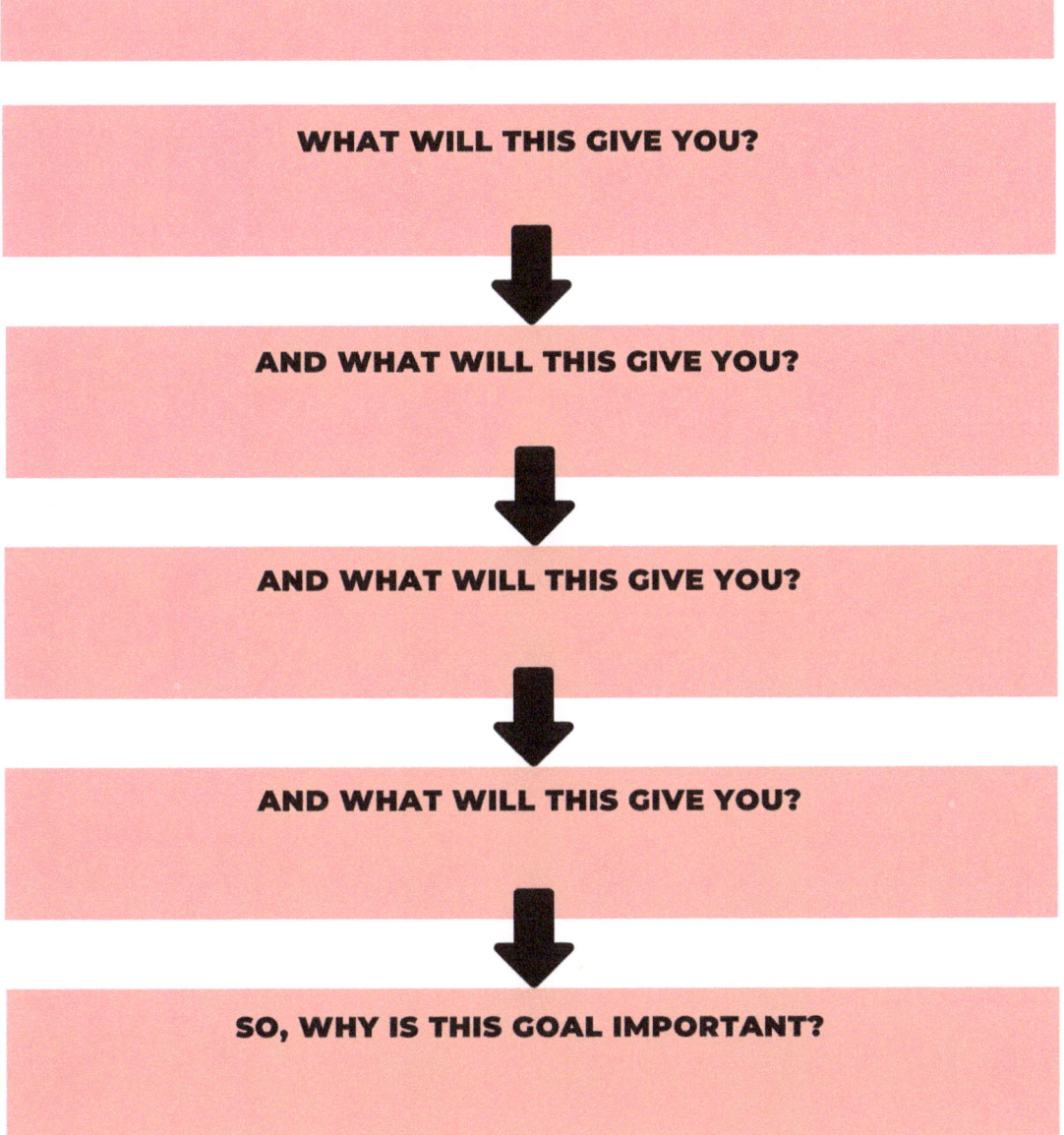

WHAT WILL THIS GIVE YOU?

⬇

AND WHAT WILL THIS GIVE YOU?

⬇

AND WHAT WILL THIS GIVE YOU?

⬇

AND WHAT WILL THIS GIVE YOU?

⬇

SO, WHY IS THIS GOAL IMPORTANT?

WHEEL OF
LIFE

As a certified coach, the wheel of life is a great tool I use with my clients to help them better understand what they can do to make their lives more balanced and fruitful. Again, your holistic life supports your professional life.

Think about these eight life categories below, and rate them from 1 - 10. Take a pencil and shade or color in your area of rating. For example, if under health, you give yourself a seven color in that portion.

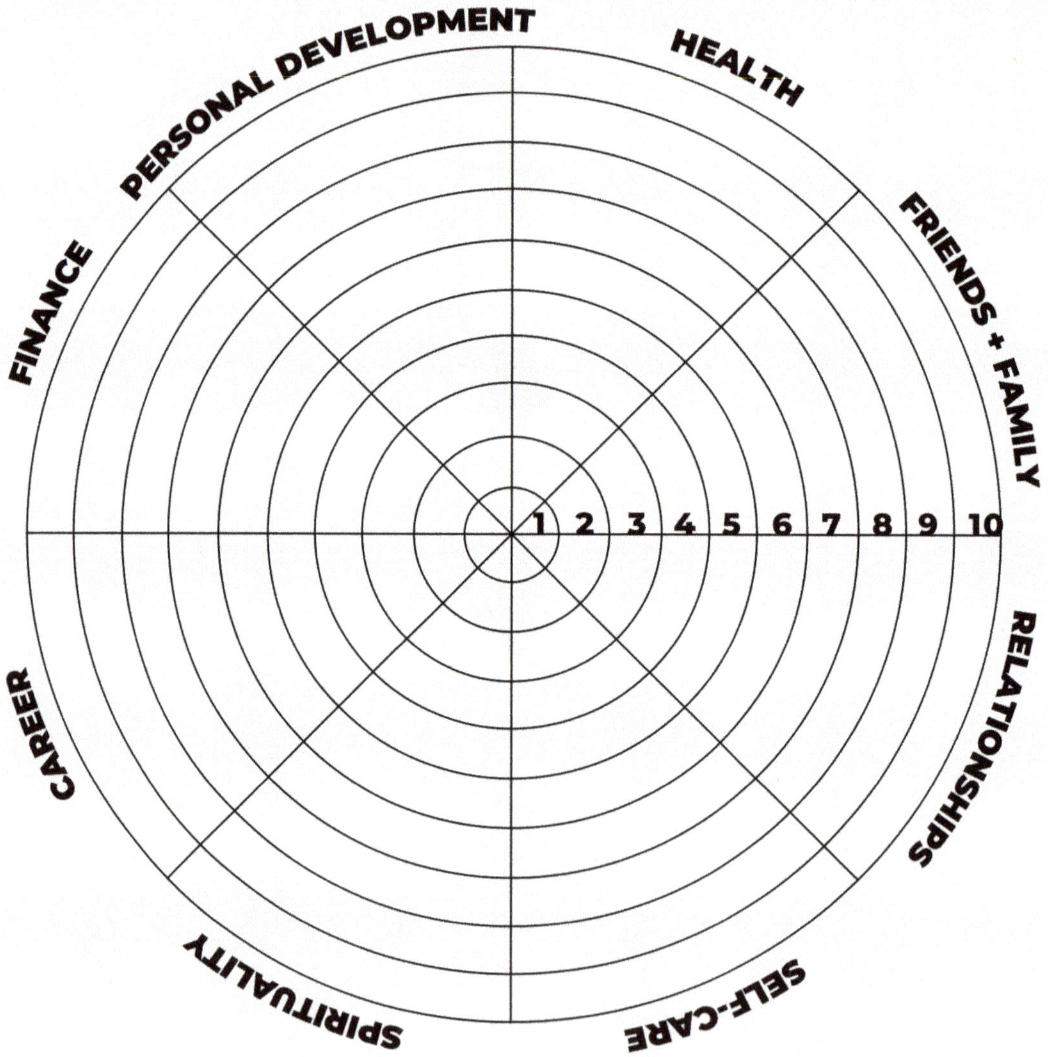

PERSONAL DEVELOPMENT

HEALTH

FINANCE

FRIENDS + FAMILY

1 2 3 4 5 6 7 8 9 10

CAREER

RELATIONSHIPS

SPIRITUALITY

SELF-CARE

RESUME + INTERVIEWING TIPS

1. RESUMES

Use action verbs and language that highlights your successes
Create different resumes for different jobs
Apply with a resume that reflects language directly from the job posting
Keep your LinkedIn updated that reflects your resume skills

2. JOB APPLYING

Leverage your communities and networks and ask them about opportunities
Consider lateral options
Create a cover letter or personal statement email to sell yourself
Keep all your professional profiles updated
Ask trusted colleagues for references

3. WHEN INTERVIEWING & AFTER

Research the people you'll interview with to find possible commonalities
Sell yourself and don't hold back
Be yourself and be honest about what you offer
Remember, you are the prize too, so it's a privilege for them to have you
Be prepared for the STAR method (see below)
Send a follow-up thanks in 1-2 days. You can reiterate skills or share any additional things you forgot to mention in your follow up

4. USE THE STAR METHOD

Have a previous job Situation example prepared
Share the Tasks you were given in previous roles
Share what Actions you took with those tasks
Be able to share the Result (good or bad) of how things went

5. ACCEPTING OR DECLINING OFFERS

Research similar titles/positions to ensure the compensation is fair
Request your worth! Counteroffer if you need to
Consider the full package benefits (EAP, 401k matching, etc.). Some of the benefits may add up to your request (if the offer amount is a little under)
Get everything in writing and your money upfront
Be able to substantiate your ask
Keep positive relationships with all recruiters even if you don't get an offer

MAKE YOUR JOB
WORK FOR YOU

STEP ONE: LEARN AS MUCH AS POSSIBLE IN YOUR ROLE (ADD VALUE, TOO) AND BUILD HEALTHY RELATIONSHIPS EVERY CHANCE YOU CAN.

STEP TWO: LOCATE 2-3 OTHER DEPARTMENTS OR ROLES (YOU'RE INTERESTED IN) AND SHADOW THOSE TO LEARN MORE SKILLS.

STEP THREE: ASK YOUR EMPLOYER TO SPONSOR CLASSES OR CERTIFICATIONS THAT ALIGN WITH YOUR POSITION OR PASSION. BE SURE TO CREATE A SOLID BASIS TO SUPPORT YOUR REQUEST FOR THEM TO PAY FOR IT. THERE IS USUALLY A BUDGET FOR ITEMS LIKE THIS; SOMETIMES, THEY WILL EVEN PAY HALF.

STEP FOUR: LEARN AS MUCH AS POSSIBLE AND FLIP ALL THOSE SKILLS LEARNED INTO A SIDE HUSTLE OR GO INTO BUSINESS FOR YOURSELF!

PROFESSIONAL DEVELOPMENT TOOLS & RESOURCES

Research 2-3 books that you will commit to reading over the next quarter. Also, identify three networking events and things you can do to build or strengthen your tribe intentionally.

READING LIST

- _____
- _____
- _____
- _____

WORKSHOP/CONFERENCE

- _____
- _____
- _____
- _____

AUTHOR'S RECOMMENDATIONS

- Woman Evolve, Sarah Jakes, Roberts
- Called to Create, Jordan Raynor
- Atomic Habits, James Clear
- The Gifts of Imperfection, Brene' Brown
- Dreams Bigger Than Texas, Rahkal C. D. Shelton

SPEAK, SIS. SPEAK!

notes

7 KEYS TO OBTAINING A MORE FULFILLING WORK EXPERIENCE

KNOW THAT YOUR SUCCESS AND FULFILLMENT IS YOUR RESPONSIBILITY. IT'S UP TO YOU, SIS!

KEY #7

IT'S NOT ENOUGH TO CREATE A PLAN AND LEARN THESE KEYS WITHOUT PUTTING THEM TO WORK. NO LIP SERVICE. YOU CAN TAKE ACTION AND GET TO WORK.

THE MOVE
GETTING TO WORK

Now it's time to get to work. Consider everything covered in this workbook and the principles learned in Woosah.

With your goals in mind, could you jot out your 6mo-1 yr plan and what you need to start or stop doing to have a more fulfilling work experience?

Everything starts with you. You are responsible for your fulfillment and success. Your disciplines, goals, actions, perspective, and mindset determine how far you'll go on this journey.

Times will be challenging, and you will certainly need to WOOSAH in every environment and often as a woman of color, but you are more than capable and equipped to be successful.

Don't expect perfection in every area; some principles will take time to grasp or implement.

The goal is to make you aware and to inspire change in your personal and professional lives. To thrive, you must gain control of situations before they control you. Be more proactive and offensive vs. reactive and defensive.

A wise person once told me that change is the only thing that truly changes. Change is constant, and since we're aware of this, it's a great time to practice being open, honest, and knowledgeable of our need for change.

If your work environment is too unbearable, impacting you physically, mentally, or emotionally, it's time to make a real change (whatever this looks like for you).

You can change your perspective and behaviors or completely change your environment if it comes to that.

Let's recap what it takes to truly have a more fulfilling work experience and get to work on our plan.

7 KEYS
FOR WORKPLACE FULFILMENT

UNDERSTANDING YOUR PURPOSE

Knowing your purpose and what you want to do provides clarity and intentional focus.

KNOWING WHAT YOU'RE UP AGAINST

As a WOC, knowing what you're up against reduces being blindsided. It provides advantages for strategic adaptability.

YOU ARE ON THE MENU & THE PRIZE!

Knowing what you offer and that you are on the menu reduces settling and short-changing yourself. There is freedom in being authentically you in the workplace.

YOU ARE A THERMOSTAT NOT A THERMOMETER

Knowing how to navigate toxic work environments, manage stress, and set boundaries is essential to your peace.

COMMUNITIES & TRIBES ARE GOLDEN!

If you want to go fast, go alone; if you want to go far, go together.

MUST HAVE A VISION, PLAN & DISCIPLINE

"You do not rise to the level of your goals. You fall to the level of your systems." -James Clear

SUCCESS & FULFILLMENT IS YOUR RESPONSIBILITY

It's not enough to create a plan and learn these keys without putting them to work. No lip service. You can take action and get to work.

WHAT WOULD MAKE YOUR WORK EXPERIENCE MORE FULFILLING?

This doesn't have to be restricted to your current profession. Think about yourself as a professional overall and identify some of your wants and needs to achieve fulfillment.

WHAT DO YOU NEED

- _____
- _____
- _____
- _____
- _____
- _____

VS

WHAT DO YOU WANT

- _____
- _____
- _____
- _____
- _____
- _____

READY? SET. GO!

SPEAK, SIS. SPEAK!
notes

SPEAK, SIS. SPEAK!

notes

SPEAK, SIS. SPEAK!
notes

SPEAK, SIS. SPEAK!

notes

SPEAK, SIS. SPEAK!
notes

SPEAK, SIS. SPEAK!
notes

SPEAK, SIS. SPEAK!

notes

SPEAK, SIS. SPEAK!

notes

SPEAK, SIS. SPEAK!
notes

SPEAK, SIS. SPEAK!
notes

SPEAK, SIS. SPEAK!
notes

SPEAK, SIS. SPEAK!

notes

SPEAK, SIS. SPEAK!

notes

SPEAK, SIS. SPEAK!

notes

SPEAK, SIS. SPEAK!

notes

SPEAK, SIS. SPEAK!
notes

SPEAKING, WORKSHOP, AND TRAINING TOPICS

Thank you for taking this journey with me! I would love to connect with your girls, employer, book club, or small groups. I aim to empower women everywhere along this road to true workplace peace via fireside chats, one-on-one coaching, and workshop training.

My background in reporting, project management, and career coaching makes me no stranger to delivering engaging and thought-provoking messages uniquely crafted just for you, sis!

Topics include, but are not limited to:

PERSONAL DEVELOPMENT & EMPOWERMENT
- Living Significantly & Operating in Excellence
- The Transilient You: Mastering Resilience During Times of Transition
- Identity Christ's: Faith, Purpose & Womanhood

PROFESSIONAL DEVELOPMENT
- HYOUman In The Workplace: Leveraging Personal Skills for Professional Success
- College & Career Readiness
- 7 Keys For Workplace Fulfillment

Rahkal Shelton Roberson

Professional Coach + Workplace Peace Advocate

www.rahkalshelton.com

FEATURES

www.ingramcontent.com/pod-product-compliance
Lightning Source LLC
Chambersburg PA
CBHW040508110526
44587CB00047B/4306